SINGAP
TRAVEL GUIDE
2022

Earth Voyage

TABLE OF CONTENTS

INTRODUCTION TO SINGAPORE
SINGAPORE'S ESSENTIALS
1. Orchard Road
2. Botanic Gardens
3. Singapore Zoo & Safari
4. The Marina Bay Region
5. Sentosa Island
SINGAPORE HISTORY

INTRODUCTION TO SINGAPORE

A Significant Asian country The melting pot of cultures. Shopping paradise. Cuisine fusion nirvana. Singapore, an island city-state with sparkling skyscrapers and unspoiled jungle, blends modernity and tradition like no other. This tiny, heavily populated tropical city-state is constantly reinventing itself. The futuristic world is a part natural marvel, and an epic dream. Gardens by the Bay looks out onto the downtown urban jungle. Singapore values its history while looking forward. Its colonial legacy is preserved in the National Gallery and the Asian Civilizations Museum, which are housed in magnificent architecture. The island is littered with melancholy World War II relics, but colorful pre-war shophouses have been revitalized as trendy stores and cafés. Singapore is full of surprises: Taoist and Hindu temples, Muslim mosques, and Christian churches coexist on the same streets as gorgeous spas and chic rooftop bars. There is never enough time to see everything Singapore has to offer, whether it's shopping for designer goods on Orchard Road, browsing booths in Chinatown, sipping a Singapore Sling at Raffles Hotel, or slurping hot laksa at an open-air hawker center. This city is replete with eye-catching festivals and events, from the Chinese New Year to the Singapore Grand Prix.

Whether you're in Singapore for a weekend or a week, our Top 10 list highlights the best of what the city-state has to offer, from the bright lights of Marina Bay to the bustling lanes of Little India. The guide includes tips throughout, such as where to find free attractions and how to avoid crowds, as well as seven easy-to-follow itineraries that will allow you to see a variety of sights in a short amount of time. Add energizing images and detailed maps, and you've got yourself an indispensable travel companion. Have fun with the material and have a great time in Singapore!

SINGAPORE is a tiny country with Greatest infrastructures, Getting to shops, parks, hotels, and tourist attractions is straightforward with an EZ-link card (which may also be used on buses) on one hand and a street map on the other. This section introduces the biggest tourist attractions in Singapore, including museums and family attractions, parks and gardens, and the Singapore River, which runs through the city's commercial district. There is a description of Singapore's multiculturalism as well as the religions practiced. Finally, there's a list of the performing arts options in this diversified Asian metropolis. Given its tiny size, Singapore features a surprising amount of museums and other places for families to explore. The museums focus on history, cultural traditions, and Asian art in general, as well as the art forms, are given by Singapore's early community of immigrants. Permanent exhibitions include Indonesian batik, Chinese porcelain and calligraphy, Malay textiles, and Peranakan jewelry. Among the other attractions are a vast zoo and one of Asia's largest bird parks. The Science Centre is ranked among the top ten in the world. Haw Par Villa, a ghastly Chinese folklore-themed theme park, is the polar opposite.

The reputation of Singapore as a successful melting pot for people of all nationalities is noteworthy in that it was achieved in such a short period of time after the island became a republic in 1965. The government has achieved great racial peace through legislation, robust public housing and education programs, and compulsory military conscription for males over the age of 18. Locals, particularly the younger generation, identify as Singaporeans first and foremost, followed by Chinese, Malays, Indians, or Eurasians.

"SINGAPORE MALAYS" refers to Malays who are descended from immigration from the Malay Peninsula. The Malay States (most notably Johore and Malacca) and the erstwhile Dutch East Indies (currently Indonesia). Bugis from Celebes, Riau Malays, Javanese, and Minang-kabau were among them. among those who (from Sumatra). The descendants of Arab migrants are known as "Singapore Malays," and They are all Muslims. Aside from the Kampong Glam enclave, which Raffles gave to the early Muslim migrants, Malays later gravitated to a number of outlying kampungs. (villages).

Malays preferred Geylang Serai, Ubi, Eunos, Bedok, Changi, and Telok Blangah. With the emergence of universal house ownership through government-built housing in the 1970s, the Malay enclaves were dismantled. During the Hari Raya holiday, the flats occupied by Malays are easily recognizable by the brilliant lights that adorn their windows. Malays are more traditional than other ethnic groups, especially when it comes to celebratory clothing. (Islamic head scarf). Indians are a heterogeneous racial group defined by their languages and religious beliefs. Tamil speakers account for around 60% of Singapore's Indian population, with origins in Tamil Nadu or the Tamil enclave in northern Sri Lanka. Other languages spoken by the Indian minority are Malayalee (8%), Punjabi, Bengali, and Telugu. According to the government, Tamil is the official language of the Indian community. Hindu holidays such as Deepavali, Thimithi, and Thaipusam, as well as the anniversaries of several Hindu deities, are the best times to experience traditional Indian culture, and Little India is the place to be.

SINGAPORE'S ESSENTIALS

Orchard Road

Singapore's national sport is shopping, and Orchard Road is the country's most prominent competitive location. What was once a desolate road flanked by spice farms and orchards is now inundated with shopping malls, department stores, and specialized shops, enough to exhaust even the most devoted shopaholic. But wait, there's more: there are food courts that will make your mouth water, as well as a heritage-listed side street crowded with bars. Before hitting the shops on Orchard Road, get a late breakfast at Kith Cafe or the historic Killiney Kopitiam. If you're looking for locally manufactured fashion labels, check out Hansel, Sects, and i.t., all of which are located within Orchardgateway. You can acquire books in the Kinokuniya bookstore in Ngee Ann City and then get lost in the modern ION Orchard Mall. Make a quick stop at Antiques of the Orient at the end of Orchard Road to look for prints. The soup dumplings, popularly known as xiao long bao, at Paradise Dynasty are wonderful, and traditional Indonesian cuisine can be found at Tambuah Mas.

Emerald Hill Road

Take a trip up frangipani-scented Emerald Hill Rd, which is bordered with some of Singapore's most exquisite terrace mansions. Special mention should be made of No. 56 (one of the first buildings here, erected in 1902), Nos. 39-45 (with extraordinarily broad frontages and a massive Chinese-style entrance gate), and Nos. 120-130 (with unusually wide frontages and a grand Chinese-style entrance gate). At the Orchard Rd end of the sloper body, a cluster of popular pubs set in handsome shophouse renovations can be found to some much-needed TLC at Tomi Foot Reflexology, Remède Spa. In the evening, toast the good life with martinis at Bar on 5, unwind with a drink at Bar Canary, or sip a drink among ancient buildings on Emerald Hill Road. Refuel at a Japanese-fusion restaurant. If you don't have a reservation at Iggy's or Buona Terra, go to it-kid Kilo Orchard or Hong Kong dumpling icon Tim Ho Wan.

Istana

The grand institutionalist residence of Singapore's president, built by the British between 1867 and 1869 as Government House, is open to the public five times a year: on Labour Day (1 May), a chosen date before National Day (7 August), Chinese New Year (January or February), Diwali (October or November), and Hari Raya Puasa (October or November) (or Eid-ul Fitr; dates vary). On certain days, you will only be able to meander through the nine-hole golf course, the beautiful terraced gardens, and a couple of the reception rooms. Bring your passport and arrive early because the line moves quickly. The strongly guarded gates are the closest you'll get the rest of the time.

Istana

Cathay Gallerye

Fans of film and romanticism will enjoy this little silver-screen museum housed in Singapore's first skyscraper. The exhibits trace the Loke family's history as early pioneers in Singapore film production and distribution and the founders of the Cathay Organisation. Vintage movie posters, cameras, and films from the golden age of local cinema are included.

Singapore River

The Singaporean River is the heart of city life, passing godowns from the 1920s, Clarke Quay's clubs and restaurants, and the skyscrapers of the financial district. The river was the first draw for the city's founder, Sir Thomas Stamford Raffles, and a stroll along its banks now provides some of the city's most iconic views. Better yet, board one of the sardine boats that used to jostle for space around Boat Quay. The river has become the emotional hub of Singapore since an intensive cleanup in 1987. It is no longer the main commercial artery, but it has shed its bad reputation.

Singapore River

Asian Museum

In 2003, the Asian Museum reopened these 1867-built ancient government offices on the riverfront.

Riverboat Tours

Traditional bumboats take about forty minutes to sail up the river, past the quays, and over Marina Bay. By the river, there are payment booths. On tourist boats, a pre-recorded tape provides tour narration. It has never been quiet since 1820 when Chinese merchants first built warehouses on the shore. The once-bustling wharf has been replaced by pubs and eateries.

Singapore River

THE SULTAN MOSQUE

Sultan Mosque is located in a neighborhood established in 1819 by the Malay Sultan of Johor, who dominated Singapore. The first mosque on this site was dedicated in 1824. It was designed in the style of a mosque found in Southeast Asia, with a low, two-tiered ceiling resembling a pyramid. The East India Company contributed to its funding. The ancient mosque had been destroyed and had to be rebuilt a century later. Swan & Maclaren, a local architectural firm responsible for a number of prominent projects, designed it. The streets surrounding the mosque are filled with booths and restaurants selling wonderful Malay delights after nightfall during Ramadan, the month of fasting. Cafés on Bussorah Street, opposite the mosque, provide Turkish or Malay tea, as well as fresh lime juice. Muslims utilize mosques for a number of purposes, including education, religious rites, and community development. These services are provided to the local Muslim community via the Sultan Mosque's expansion, which was built in 1993. Non-Muslims are welcome to attend the mosque, although they should avoid the main prayer hall. Viewing is permitted from the adjacent courtyard and hallways, though. Appropriate apparel, such as slacks or long skirts and sleeved shirts, is required. Visitors who arrive in inappropriate attire are handed robes at the mosque's entrance.

THE SULTAN MOSQUE

BOTANIC GARDENS

This park is a UNESCO World Heritage Site and one of the most stunning botanical gardens in Southeast Asia. The park, originally opened as a pleasure garden in 1859, contains walkways that snake through a tropical environment that highlights the region's natural habitats and species. There are avenues of frangipani and scarlet lipstick palms, as well as expansive, sloping lawns with trees and sculptures. On weekends, the park is packed with families, joggers, and dog walkers, but during the week, it is a calm retreat. Note That Entrance to the National Orchid Garden is $5 for adults, $5 for seniors, and free for children from 8 a.m. to 7 p.m. The Shaw Foundation Symphony Stage hosts free outdoor events on weekends.

National Orchid Garden

The entrance of this magnificent enclosure first opened in 1995. This collection contains over 1,000 orchid species and 2,000 hybrids. Some hybrids bear the names of visiting leaders of state and dignitaries from all over the world. It is the only garden that requires a fee to enter.

National Orchid Garden

Great Lakes

The gardens have three lakes. Swan Lake got its name from the white swans that live there, whereas ducks and black swans live in Eco Lake. Outdoor shows are held on a stage in the middle of Symphony Lake.

Rain Forest

The park's early organizers understood the importance of the native forest and preserved a piece of it, where ancient trees thrive today.

Rain Forest

SINGAPORE ZOO & SAFARI

The Singapore Zoo, as well as its Night Safari and River Safari offshoots, are three adjacent attractions where tourists can see hundreds of animals in their natural habitats. The Night Safari is very popular since it allows visitors to observe nocturnal animals at their most active. The River Safari is a zoo and aquarium dedicated to the wildlife of the world's main rivers, including the Nile, Mississippi, and Yangtze. Through interactive exhibits, performances, and English-language programs, visitors can learn about the animals and their behavior. 80 Mandai Lake Rd., 6269 3411 Zoo, open everyday from 8:30 am to 6 pm, admission S$33 for adults and S$22 for children Night Safari is available daily from 7:15 p.m. to midnight and costs S$45 for adults and S$30 for kids. Open everyday from 10 a.m. to 7 p.m., River Safari costs S$30 for adults and S$20 for kids. Public transportation from the city center to the zoo can take up to an hour. Private bus companies provide transportation to the zoo from a number of downtown hotels and attractions.

Activities

Amazon River Adventure The watercraft excursion on the River Safari takes you past Amazonian animal cages, including Brazilian tapirs and scarlet ibises. Breakfast in the Wilderness Breakfast is a favorite activity at the zoo, where visitors may interact with active orangutans and other friendly animals. This is also an excellent time to visit the zoo because the weather is still beautiful and the exhibits are not overcrowded. Vulnerable Forest This area in the zoo, housed in a giant biodome, resembles a rain forest for ring-tailed lemurs, sloths, flying foxes, and other animals. Visitors are welcome to see them as they go about their daily activities.

SINGAPORE ZOO I

ZOO Tips

The Singapore Zoo, Night Safari, and River Safari are all located near to each other. Singapore Wildlife Reserves administers them all. While strolling around the zoo is the best way to observe it, a tram that charges a fee is also available. Visitors to the Night Safari can also ride a tram, albeit this is not included in the park admission ticket. It takes tourists on a fun circular circuit with various stops where they can get off and explore the terrain.

SINGAPORE SAFARI

The Marina Bay region

The Marina Bay area, which was developed on reclaimed land and formed a freshwater reservoir in the process, offers breathtaking views of the cityscape. Marina Bay includes green spaces such as Gardens by the Bay, shopping malls, and luxury residential high-rises, as well as expanding Singapore's banking sector. Moshe Safdie's massive boat-shaped building on top of the Marina Bay Sands resort is the most eye-catching, but there are many other bizarre architectural marvels. You may walk around the entire Bay on a 2-mile (3.5-kilometer) beachside promenade with pedestrian bridges. Open daily from 8:30 a.m. to 10:00 p.m., Singapore Flyer is located at 30 Raffles Avenue and can be reached at 6333 3311. Children (3-12 years old) pay S$21 instead of S$33. 18 Marina Gardens Drive, Gardens by the Bay, pen daily from 5 a.m. to 2 a.m.; conservatories open from 9 a.m. to 9 p.m.; cost: S$28 for adults and S$15 for kids; marina barrage, 8 Marina Gardens Drive, 6514 5959; open daily from 9 a.m. to 9 p.m. Wednesday-\sMonday The casino at Marina Bay Sands is free for visitors from other countries. There is a smart casual dress code; swimming suits, shorts, and flip-flops are not acceptable. At MBS' two theaters, musicals and traveling Broadway productions are presented, offering top-notch family entertainment.

Helix Bridge

The structure of DNA influenced the design of this curved steel pedestrian bridge that connects Marina South and Marina Center. Its observation platforms offer breathtaking views of the Bay, particularly of the Art Science Museum, and it is illuminated at night.

Helix Bridge

Singapore Flyer

The tallest spinning wheel in the entire world stands 541 feet (165 meters) over Marina Bay. It offers expansive views of the Singapore River that stretch from the Colonial District to the far-off nearby islands. Three opulent options are available for an unforgettable Flyer experience. The Premium Champagne Flight and the Singapore Sling Flight come with an alcoholic beverage. Two spins of the wheel and a four-course Western, Chinese, or vegetarian meal are included with the Premium Sky Dining Flight.

Singapore Flyer

Singapore Flyer

The Merlion

The Merlion symbolizes the unity of the lion city and the sea. (half-fish & half-lion) The current statue, which looks like an ancient mythological beast standing guard over the Singapore River, was unveiled in 1972.

The Merlion

RAFFLES HOTEL

Behind her famed façade, Singapore's grandest old lady lurks a labyrinth of tropical gardens and verandas. The Raffles Hotel was founded in 1887 by the Armenian Sarkies brothers in a beachside bungalow. It was saved from demolition by being named a National Monument during its centennial year, and multimillion-dollar upgrades ensure that the hotel preserves its colonial elegance. Raffles is a destination in and of itself, with its restaurants, boutiques, galleries, bars, and museum. Despite the fact that character and opulence are expensive, few hotels can match Raffles' blend of history, grandeur, and colonial ambiance. The hotel's famous, exotically dressed Sikh doormen are kind and agreeable to photo requests. After three years and S$160 million in renovations, the modern Raffles Hotel opened in 1991. Additional renovations have preserved the hotel's standing as the grand dame of Singapore's luxury hotels more than 25 years later. The Prolonged Bar As the home of the Singapore Sling, this must be the only pub in town where drinkers are encouraged to trash peanut shells.

The Raffles Gin of 1915 To honor the 100th anniversary of the Singapore Sling, this gin was created in collaboration with the London-based microdistillery Sipsmith, whose co-founder was a descendent of Stamford Raffles. courthouse raffles The Italian food served in this outdoor restaurant, which is surrounded by palm trees, is the perfect place to experience the elegant and peaceful ambiance of the hotel. All of Raffles' restaurants uphold excellent standards, but Raffles Grill stands out as the most elegant. Raffles' guests include authors, actors, and musicians of all ages. Early guests included Joseph Conrad and Rudyard Kipling, who was followed by Somerset Maugham. Anthony Burgess stayed in Singapore on his route to Malaya in the 1950s. Noel Coward, Ava Gardner, and Elizabeth Taylor succeeded Charlie Chaplin and Maurice Chevalier in the years following World War II.

RAFFLES HOTEL

SENTOSA ISLAND

Sentosa is Singapore's pleasure island, a recreation destination. There is something for everyone here, including award-winning spa resorts, golf courses, and a marina. A plethora of taverns and restaurants are located around the area's attractive manmade beaches, which are adjacent to green wooded slopes. The island was previously known as Pulau Blakang Mati, which translates to "death from behind," most likely due to pirate raids on its coasts. Later, it was renamed Sentosa, which means "calmness." Entrance is S$1; if you drive to Sentosa, you must pay a flat fee that varies depending on the time of your visit. Tanjong Beach has the best sunset views on the island. Coasts, which surrounds Siloso Beach, offers a variety of dining options, serving drinks and foreign cuisine all day.

Siloso Beach

Charming young people who lounge and play volleyball visit this beach. Several beach bars and shops are open during the day, but the pace and level of noise pick up after dark.

Siloso Beach

Sentosa 4D Adventure Land

Adventure Land is Named Southeast Asia's first 4D cinema. modern digital projection system, surround sound, and seats that move in sync with the event on the screen Mist spray is one of the impacts. scenes involving water

singapore universal

S.E.A. Aquarium

The highlight of the aquarium's huge tanks is the Open Ocean region, which is home to sharks and manta rays. Especially accessible is the Maritime Experiential Museum.

S.E.A. Aquarium

Cable Car

The cable car's glass cabins offer a costly yet exhilarating way to travel from Mount Faber to Sentosa. A branch line from Imbiah Lookout stops at the island's westernmost point.

Cable car

Singapore History

In February 1819, Sir Thomas Stamford Raffles made an agreement with a local Malay ruler that allowed the East India Company to establish a trading post in Singapore. The island was a British colony until 1959. Singapore became a republic in August 1965, after a brief spell as part of Malaysia beginning in 1963. Singapore's history, on the other hand, extends back far further in time and reflects the power shifts in Southeast Asia over the last few centuries. The island, which is just 42 kilometers (25 miles) long and 23 kilometers (14 miles) wide, is located near the Malay Peninsula's southernmost tip, on an important marine trade route connecting the South China Sea, the Indian Ocean, and the Spice Islands. Prior to the arrival of the British, Singapore was successively ruled by Sailendra (Sumatra), Majapahit (Java), Siam, and Malacca, which helped to establish it as a significant trade hub. Numerous geographical references hint that an important trading post formerly stood on Singapore or one of the nearby islands. The Greek Ptolemy built an emporium (a trade center for goods from both the East and the West) called Sabana close to what is now Singapore in the second century. Marco Polo mentioned "Chiamassie," which may have been "Temasek," Singapore's name from the 13th century, while the Chinese named a "island at the end of the peninsula," or "Pu-Luo-Chung," in the third century.

Beginning in the seventh century, kingdoms with bases on the Indonesian islands of Sumatra and Java wielded political and commercial dominance in Southeast Asia. These kingdoms' strength stemmed on their control of the sea passages connecting India and China, as well as the trade in spices such as pepper, nutmeg, cinnamon, and cloves, which were highly valued in both China and Europe. In 1279, the Majapahit empire was established in Java. Thailand dominated over the Malay Peninsula, while Sumatra, Java, and Borneo were under its control. A few years later, the balance of power shifted, and Javanese court documents from 1365 mention a vassal kingdom called "Temasek." The Majapahit had lost control of the region by the end of the century. Around 1390, Iskandar, a Palembang king, was driven from the city and took refuge in Temasek. Here, he gained leadership before being eventually driven out, possibly by Thai attackers. Iskandar later founded the Malacca sultanate, which gradually expanded its control over Temasek. The term "Singapura" has its origins shrouded in myth. According to the Sejarah Melayu (Malay Annals), the Sumatran king Sang Nila Utama renamed Temasek to "Singapura." Utama accidentally came into a strange monster on an island after escaping a shipwreck. The king gave the island the name Singapore, which translates to "Lion City," after discovering that it was a lion.

European powers wanted control of territory in Asia early in the fifteenth century to have direct access to the lucrative spice trade. In 1511, the Portuguese conquered Ma- lacca. The Dutch took possession of the Indonesian islands, which became known as the Dutch East Indies, in 1641. The defeated Malacca sultanate maintained control over Singapore from Johore. The British East India Company began to challenge the Dutch East India Company's dominance in the Indonesian Archipelago in the nineteenth century. The British constructed a base in Penang, at the northern end of the Malacca Strait. One of the British East India Company's most ambitious and forward-thinking officers was Thomas Stamford Raffles. Raffles held the position of lieutenant governor of the Dutch possessions in Java from 1811 until 1816, when the British acquired control of them. This was following the defeat of the French and their Dutch allies in the Napoleonic Wars. Although Java was given to the Dutch in 1816, Raffles had grand intentions to increase British influence there. He set off from Penang in the early months of 1819 with a small expeditionary force. At that time, the Johore royal family ruled over a small group of orang laut (sea people) who resided at the mouth of the Singapore River.

Raffles arrived in Singapore on February 6, 1819, and signed a treaty with the Malay emperor. Raffles was barely in Singapore for a week, but he decided that there was a safe anchorage and made the critical decision to declare Singapore as a tax-free port. Colonel William Farquhar was given power by Raffles, who encouraged settlers and commerce vessels to use the new port. Trade expanded rapidly. Raffles instituted stronger urban development limitations on his second visit, a month later, which still regulate the appearance of Singapore's older neighborhoods. Each neighborhood and hamlet has its own local government. There are still Chinese, Indian, and Kampong Glam enclaves in Chinatown and Serangoon Road, respectively (Malaysians). According to British East India Company ideology, streets were laid out with "five foot ways" (covered walkways or corridors). The Singapore River swiftly emerged as the most convenient economic hub, and "godowns"—warehouses—were built to safeguard goods while they were being trans-shipped. Before leaving the East in 1822, Raffles went back to Singapore for another six months of leadership. He passed away there.

It took six months for news of Raffles' foundation of Singapore as a trading post to reach London, and his claims were vehemently contested by the Dutch, but Singapore's early success in drawing trade thrilled the British authorities. Eventually, in 1824, the Anglo-Dutch Treaty partitioned area around the Malacca Straits, with the British East India Company controlling Penang, Malacca, and Singapore, which became known collectively as the Straits Settlements in 1826.

Singapore's rapid growth drew merchants, traders, and laborers to the port. The population increased from less than 1,000 in 1819 to sixteen thousand in 1836 and eighty-one thousand in 1869. The majority of the immigrants were Chinese men brought as indentured servants, but there were also European businessmen and bureaucrats, as well as many Indian soldiers and Malay indigenous. These ethnic groups formed the backbone of Singapore's diverse society. Singapore has evolved into a world-class port. As a British East India Company colony, there was little governance and rampant chaos. Trade fluctuated greatly, and piracy was a continual menace. Despite the challenges, Chinese merchants Tan Chee Sang and Whampoa, who both operated out of sizable estates on the banks of the Singapore River, were among those who prospered and left their mark. Prosperous merchants lived in huge estates on the nearby hills. The streets Orchard Road, Orange Grove Road, and Nutmeg Road are named for regionally grown crops. To cope with Chinese secret organizations and oversee the welfare of Chinatown's Chinese community, the colonial government formed a Chinese Protectorate in 1877 under the direction of William Pickering.

Timber constructions gave way to stone and brick building in Singapore's early days. Private dwellings, massive warehouses, and places of worship were built. Rows of shophouses lined the streets of Chinatown and the primary business sector south of the river, which surrounded Raffles Place. The 1826 Parliament House part, the 1835 Armenian Church, the 1841 Caldwell House in Chijmes, and the 1841 Thian Hock Keng shrine are all still standing. Unlike Chinatown, which is extremely congested, there is plenty of room in this region. In the 1860s, Singapore began a new era of wealth. In 1867, Straits Settlements was recognized as a British Crown colony. Singapore's position as a significant port was cemented with the construction of the Suez Canal in 1869, ensuring its central role within the British empire. With Harry St. George Ord as its first governor, Singapore became the colony's administrative hub. The Supreme Court on the Padang and Government House, two spectacular colonial buildings, served as the offices of the administration (now the Istana). The employment of steamships expanded dramatically in the latter half of the nineteenth century, replacing traditional trade in exotic products and spices with trade in tin, rubber, oil, copra, and sugar; English and Chinese interests predominated.

In 1902, a gas storage facility was built on Pulau Bukom, and Singapore became the Far East's oil distribution hub. Tanjong Pagar's port facilities have been renovated, and a new pier has been built.

During World War I many Germans were imprisoned at the Teutonia Club, which is now the Goodwood Park Hotel, The only notable instance happened in 1915 when Indian Sepoy troops guarding captured German prisoners staged a brief insurrection. Despite successive slumps in rubber, tin, and oil, Tan Kah Kee and Lee Kong Chian, who traded in rubber, and Aw Boon Haw, who developed the Haw Par Gardens and traded in Tiger Balm, a Chinese medicine, built fortunes in the years following the war. Unrestricted immigration of destitute young men from South China proceeded unabated. Chinese supporters of Sun Yat Sen organized violent rallies in 1919, and Chinese-medium schools became a focal point for Chinese patriotic fervor. In the 1920s, as communist power grew in China, Chinese immigration was prohibited, and Chinese schools were closed.

The loss of the British in Singapore and Malaya during World War II, which undermined notions of British colonial power, marked a turning point in Singapore's history. British military authority had left Singapore since it had insufficient fortifications and no chance of receiving reinforcements because they were fighting in Europe. Within a few weeks following the Japanese invasion of Malaya, the Japanese easily took control of Singapore.

In 1942, Singapore was renamed Syonan-To ("Southern Light"). European citizens and prisoners of war were housed in Changi Prison and other camps. The railway in Burma was built at a heavy human cost. The Japanese civilian populace was terrified of the kempetai (secret police) and famine. The kempetai massacred Chinese people several times. Elections were held in 1955 to approve a new constitution, which went into force in 1957. Since 1959, when it won the majority of seats in the polls, the PAP has won every election.

In an uneasy alliance to win independence from the United Kingdom in 1963, Singapore and Malaya joined forces. On August 9, 1965, Singapore was expelled from Malaysia and forced to create an independent country. Despite being admitted to the United Nations and the Commonwealth of Nations, Singapore's RETURN OF THE UK The Japanese gave up after being bombarded in 1945 at Hiroshima and Nagasaki. After the British left, Singapore was given back to civil rule as a Crown Colony. But the residents of Malaya and Singapore were no longer content to live under foreign rule. Even while British rule remained in place until 1959, there was a lot of pressure for independence. Actually, a transfer of power to Singapore was being prepared, and MPs were working with the British on a new constitution.

Singapore was a dirty, filthy, overcrowded city after WWII, with a thriving black market. Despite the emergence of political parties and the registration of voters in the 1950s, the slow pace of change resulted in continuing local unhappiness. The People's Action Party (PAP) was founded in 1955, led by Lee Kuan Yew, a lawyer with a Cambridge education. The little island's leadership was faced with the challenge of preserving its economic survival. Singapore remained a major trading port with banking, shipping, and storage capabilities, but this was insufficient for future growth. The British announced the withdrawal of their military presence, which had contributed 20% of the country's GDP, in 1967. But Singapore, working with international companies, quickly industrialized and found new opportunities. After four years, the economy was booming.

In less than 200 years, Singapore has transformed itself from a backwater to one of the world's "economic wonders." Former Singapore Prime Minister Lee Kuan Yew deserves recognition. Lee, who retired in 1990, supervised Singapore's transformation from an island state devoid of natural resources to the industrialized nation it is today. Policies focusing on stability and productivity are shaped by tough and corrupt-free leadership. National defense, education, housing, infrastructure, public order, industrialization, and modernization have all been prioritized. Singapore's GDP has grown at an annual rate of 9% on average since independence. Over 90% of the population is now literate, and more than 85% own their own home. The surroundings of Singapore have also seen significant alteration. Its size has increased by 10% over the past 30 years as a result of land reclamation on its southern side. The majority of the roughly 4 million residents live in high-rise apartments constructed by the government, and many of the older buildings have been razed and rebuilt with tall, air-conditioned offices and hotels. Given its small size and precarious beginnings, Singapore is currently preparing for the new information technology-based global economy and playing an outsized role on the world's financial and political stage.

THE END

Printed in Great Britain
by Amazon